50 THINGS YOU SHOULD KNOW ABOUT TITANIC

by Sean Callery

QEB

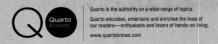

Quarto is the authority on a wide range of topics.
Quarto educates, entertains and enriches the lives of
our readers—enthusiasts and lovers of hands-on living.
www.quartoknows.com

Design and Editorial: Tall Tree Ltd
Consultant: Dr Eric Kentley

Published in the United States by
QEB Publishing, Inc.
6 Orchard
Lake Forest, CA 92630

A CIP record for this book is available
from the Library of Congress.

ISBN 978 1 68297 023 2

Printed in China

Words in **bold** are explained
in the glossary on page 78.

CONTENTS

INTRODUCTION

The sinking of *Titanic* is one of the best-known tragedies of the 20th century. It was the largest and most luxurious liner at a time when the only way to cross the Atlantic was by sea. Designed to be safe and comfortable, it sank on its first voyage within three hours of hitting an **iceberg**. It is estimated that more than 1,500 people lost their lives.

FLOATING TOWN

Titanic was like an enormous floating town with room for 3,547 people: 905 passengers in **first class**, 564 in **second class**, 1,134 in **third class**, plus 944 crew members. It was called the "Ship of Dreams" because it was carrying many migrants escaping poverty in Europe for a new life in the USA. Other travelers on board included rich Americans returning from European holidays.

▲ A 1909 ad for trips aboard Titanic, which was still being built at the time.

▼ RMS Titanic sets sail from Southampton on April 10, 1912.

NO NEED TO WORRY

Elisabeth Allan was traveling first class with her aunt. Her aunt's maid, Emilie Kreuchen, had a cheaper third-class cabin. Elizabeth wrote that after *Titanic* struck the iceberg, Emilie came to her and said: "'Miss Allen, the baggage room is full of water.' I replied she needn't worry...and it would be all right for her to go back to her cabin. She went back and returned to us immediately to say her cabin was flooded."

Across the world, people were shocked when they heard about the *Titanic* disaster. They had come to believe that the giant liners of the age were simply too technologically advanced to sink. The tragedy led to a wide range of safety improvements for ocean liners.

▼ After the disaster, stunned people wait for news at the offices of White Star, the owners of Titanic.

▼ Titanic's *sister ship*, Olympic.

HEROES

The *Titanic* story is filled with heroes. There were men who realized there was no way for them to get off the sinking ship, but they helped others to escape, then waited to die with dignity. But others were accused of jumping aboard **lifeboats** as they were lowered, and even offering bribes to the lifeboat crew to ensure their own safety.

▼ Titanic lifeboats gathered in New York after the sinking. More passengers would have survived had there been enough lifeboats for everyone on board.

JUST UNLUCKY

Titanic's sister ship, *Olympic*, had the same design and continued to sail until 1935— its crew gave it the nickname "Old Reliable." So *Titanic* was unlucky. The iceberg it hit did not make one large hole (which the ship could have survived), but ripped its **hull** in several places. This also happened in a remote part of the Atlantic, and there were very few ships nearby which could have come to help in the short time it took *Titanic* to sink.

The age of liners

1

When *Titanic* was built, there was a huge demand for ships that could carry people across the Atlantic Ocean. Companies competed to build the largest and most luxurious ships possible.

BIGGER AND FASTER

In the 19th century, more and more people wanted to cross the Atlantic, but the journey took weeks. So ship building companies developed new technologies and built bigger and faster ships. Wooden sail-driven ships gave way to iron-hulled steamships, powered first by paddles and later by propellers and **turbine engines**. This cut the journey time from weeks to days.

TOO MUCH, TOO SOON

The story of the *SS Great Eastern* shows the problems shipping firms faced in the mid-19th century. Designed by Isambard Kingdom Brunel, and launched in 1858, the liner was 682 feet long—six times larger than any other ship of the time—and could carry 4,000 passengers. But it was too big for most harbors, so it could not cover many routes and was not very successful commercially. Brunel had created a ship that was simply too advanced for its time.

▲ *Isambard Kingdom Brunel, the designer of the* SS Great Eastern.

KEY EVENTS

1845
The *SS Great Britain* is the first iron steamer to cross the Atlantic, powered by the new propeller technology. It takes 14 days (see above).

1845
White Star, the shipping line that will order the construction of *Titanic*, is established in Liverpool, England (see page 10).

1869
The shipbuilders Harland & Wolff are given the contract for all White Star ships including *Titanic* (see page 11).

An 1875 ad for Cunard's regular service between Liverpool and New York.

RIVALS

In 1912, there were four main companies running regular passenger services from Europe to America: White Star and Cunard in Britain, and their German rivals Norddeutscher Lloyd (NDL) and Hamburg America. Some competed for speed. Others, like White Star, aimed for comfort and style, as with *Titanic*. All had to balance the need to appeal to rich vacationers (who expected to be treated like top hotel guests) and poor **emigrants** traveling to North America, who made up most of the passengers.

RADIO

Developed by Italian inventor Guglielmo Marconi, **radio** technology was fairly new in 1912 and only a few ships, including *Titanic*, carried equipment that allowed them to communicate across the sea. In 1910, radio helped to capture a murderer called Hawley Harvey Crippen who had boarded the *SS Montrose* to escape Britain. The captain recognized him and sent a radio message. British police caught a faster liner, *Laurentic*, and were waiting for Crippen when he arrived in Canada. He was later hanged.

◄ Launched in 1906, Cunard's RMS Mauretania *was the fastest liner plying the route across the Atlantic.*

1892
The US government establishes the Ellis Island processing center to deal with the millions of **immigrants** arriving from Europe every year (see page 8).

1907
Shipping firm Cunard's *Mauretania* sets a new speed record of 4 days and 19 hours for crossing the Atlantic Ocean (see above).

1907
White Star and Harland & Wolff decide to build two huge new **transatlantic** liners: *Olympic* and the world's biggest ship, *Titanic* (see page 11).

Emigration

In 1820, there were **9.6 million** people living in the USA. By 1910, this figure had risen almost ten times to **92.2 million**, mainly through people moving there from other parts of the world. The USA welcomed new people to work in its factories and grow food for its expanding population.

THIRD-CLASS TRAVEL

Most emigrants were poor and could only afford to travel third class. Many were single men looking to make their fortune or families hoping to start new lives. On board, they often had to stay in cramped conditions with poor food. But third class on *Titanic* was like a palace compared to some liners.

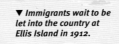
▼ Immigrants wait to be let into the country at Ellis Island in 1912.

EMIGRATION CAUSES

Unrest and suffering across Europe led many to try for a new life in the USA or Canada. Causes included shortages of land to farm, lack of jobs, and religious and political problems. In Ireland, the failure of the potato crop in 1845 led to a famine, forcing 1.5 million people to leave there for America.

▼ Map showing the number of people who emigrated from Europe to the USA in 1901–1910.

NORWAY
SWEDEN
RUSSIA
IRELAND
ENGLAND
PRUSSIA & GERMAN STATES
POLAND
AUSTRIA
FRANCE
ITALY
SPAIN

■ 300,000   600,000
2,000,000

▼ In the 62 years it was open, more than 12 million people passed through Ellis Island before it was closed in 1954.

ELLIS ISLAND

The US government set up a base on Ellis Island in New York Bay in 1892 to receive immigrants. Here, officials interviewed third-class passengers and checked them for diseases. Around 98 percent were allowed into the country.

Millionaire travel

Many of the first-class passengers on board *Titanic* were rich Americans who were returning from vacations abroad and wanted to travel in as luxurious and comfortable a way as possible.

▲ First-class passengers aboard an early 20th-century luxury liner.

TOP-CLASS TRAVEL

Wealthy Americans took vacations across the world as a sign of their status. It showed they were rich enough not to have to work all the time, and refined enough to visit other countries and enjoy their culture and history.

LUXURY HOTEL

The shipping companies promoted their ships by comparing them to luxury hotels with fantastic facilities. Traveling first class on a liner also offered rich travelers the chance to meet other wealthy people for business or pleasure.

▲ The first-class dining room of the SS König Albert, a German luxury liner.

The shipping line

White Star Line planned for *Titanic* to be one of three near-identical ships that would bring luxury to transatlantic voyages. The ships were a massive investment, but the firm believed it could make the money back through ticket sales to rich and poor customers traveling from Southampton, UK, to New York every Wednesday.

BUST AND BOOM

White Star was set up in 1845, running trips to Australia where there was a **gold rush** at the time. After the firm went bust in 1868, it was bought by shipping **magnate** Thomas Ismay, who turned it into a transatlantic steamship company.
It prospered for 31 years until he died, when his son Joseph Bruce Ismay took over the company. In 1902, it was taken over by the International Mercantile Marine company, led by American banker J. P. Morgan, but Ismay stayed in charge.

◀ *One of the wealthiest men on Earth, and the owner of White Star, J. P. Morgan was due to travel on* Titanic, *but canceled at the last minute.*

SPEEDY RIVALS

White Star's major rivals, Cunard and the German line NDL, built superfast ships, but White Star had a different strategy. Instead of speedy travel (which often meant an uncomfortable journey as the ships vibrated so much), it promised luxury for first-class travelers and comfort for all. This meant treating third-class passengers much better than other shipping lines by offering superior food and cabins for families.

▲ *Built in 1901, the SS Kronprinz Wilhelm was one of the fastest ships of the day.*

The shipbuilders

Founded in 1861, Harland & Wolff had grown to become one of the biggest shipbuilders in the world. Its **dockyard** in Belfast, Ireland, was the city's main employer. The firm was unusual for the time as it not only designed, built, and launched ships, but also made many of the interior fittings on site.

THE CHAIRMAN

William Pirrie started at Harland & Wolff as a 15-year-old apprentice in 1862, working in the drawing office. He learned how ships were designed and built as he rose through the ranks to become chairman in 1895. He toured the workyard every day, checking on every tiny detail.

▼ *Together, the chairmen of White Star, J. Bruce Ismay (left), and of Harland & Wolff, Willian Pirrie (right), oversaw* Titanic's *construction.*

PLANNING THE FUTURE

From 1869 onward, Harland & Wolff had an agreement to build all White Star ships. The chairmen of both companies, William Pirrie and J. Bruce Ismay, devised a plan in 1907 to build two of the largest liners ever to service the transatlantic route. Known as *Olympic* and *Titanic*, the ships would be built at the same time. A third was later added to the list. Initially called *Gigantic*, its name was subsequently changed to *Britannic*.

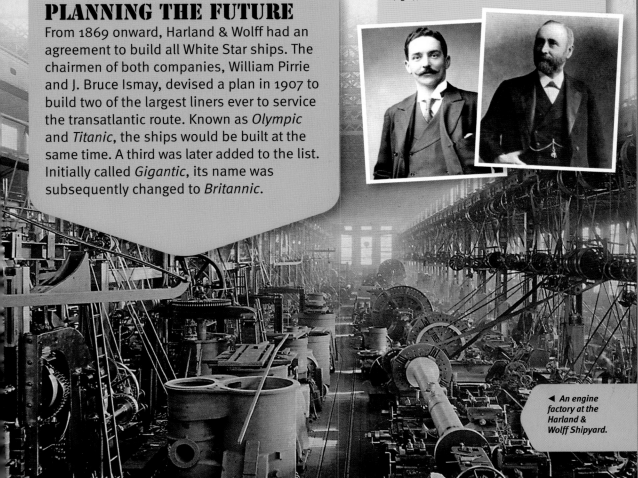

◄ *An engine factory at the Harland & Wolff Shipyard.*

6

Titanic plans

In the early 20th century, ship designs were drawn painstakingly by hand. Every detail of *Titanic* first appeared as a set of lines on paper in Harland & Wolff's drafting department. Later, these plans were turned into reality a short distance away at the dockyard.

BUSY MAN

Thomas Andrews joined Harland & Wolff in 1889 at the age of 16. He spent time in many departments during his apprenticeship, eventually learning every stage of how ships were constructed. By 1907, he was managing director of the drafting department, but he often toured the site to check on the progress of work, sometimes having lunch with the men building the ships. He was a very well-known and popular person in the shipyard.

▲ *Thomas Andrews, designer of* Titanic.

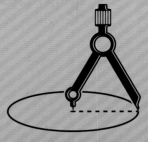

JOINT CREATORS

The two men who were chiefly responsible for the design of *Titanic* were both related to William Pirrie. The first was Pirrie's brother-in-law, Alexander Carlisle. He worked all his life for Harland & Wolff and drew up the initial designs, including deciding on the number of lifeboats. When he left this role, Pirrie's nephew, Thomas Andrews, took over.

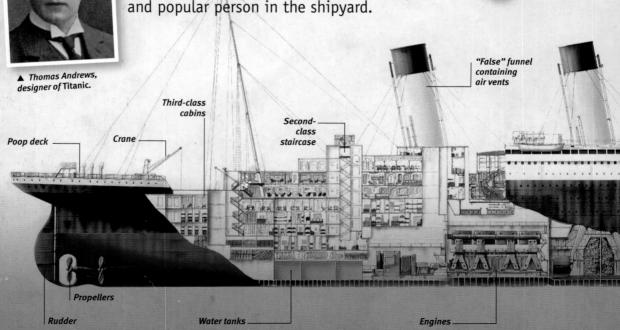

Poop deck

Crane

Third-class cabins

Second-class staircase

"False" funnel containing air vents

Propellers

Rudder

Water tanks

Engines

A COMFORTABLE VOYAGE

Titanic was designed to be comfortable for all passengers. The first-class cabins were enormous, while the second and third-class alternatives were still pretty spacious for the time. The design included plenty of public spaces where people could gather. This meant that *Titanic* could only carry the same number of passengers as smaller ships—but the passengers would have more space to stretch their legs, and would travel in comfort.

▲ *Titanic's first-class lounge was luxuriously decorated and furnished.*

WATERTIGHT WALLS

Titanic's key safety feature was a series of 16 compartments with watertight walls at the bottom of the ship. It was thought that even if water got in, it could not flow far, as it would be trapped within the walls. The walls rose as high as E Deck (see below) but, crucially, they had no roofs, which meant that water could flow over them.

FOUR BUT NO MORE

Thomas Andrews calculated that *Titanic* would stay afloat even if four of its 16 watertight compartments flooded. This led many people to believe that *Titanic* was virtually unsinkable.

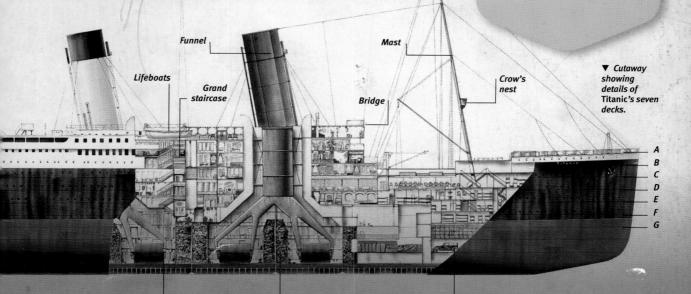

Funnel

Mast

Lifeboats

Grand staircase

Bridge

Crow's nest

▼ *Cutaway showing details of Titanic's seven decks.*

A
B
C
D
E
F
G

Boiler

Coal bunker

Cargo hold

Constructing *Titanic*

The hugely ambitious task of building *Olympic* and *Titanic* required careful planning. Harland & Wolff took on more workers, calculating that it would take 3,000 men, working six days a week, two years to put *Titanic* together, piece by piece.

Titanic's rudder was almost 80 feet high and weighed about 110 tons.

THE PROCESS

First, the ship was designed, deck by deck and room by room. Then a list was made of every single item needed to build it. If Harland & Wolff could make an item on site, they did— from beds to funnels. If not, it was shipped in—for example, the main anchor and chain were forged at Dudley in the West Midlands of England, and then transported to Belfast.

▶ *A replica of one of Titanic's giant anchors. Each weighed about 17 tons.*

▼ *The twin giants, Olympic (left) and Titanic (right), photographed on March 6, 1912, a month before Titanic's maiden voyage.*

KEY EVENTS

March 1909
The construction of *Titanic* begins at Harland & Wolff with the laying down of the **keel** (see page 16).

May 31, 1911
With the metal plating now riveted onto the framework, the empty hull is launched (see pages 18–19).

June 1911
Titanic is towed to the fitting-out basin so that its engines and boilers can be installed (see page 19).

October 1911
Tickets go on sale. Those in first, second, and third class can expect different levels of comfort (see pages 22–29).

A Harland & Wolff plaque installed on the Nomadic, *a support boat for* Titanic. *It is now the only remaining White Star ship in existence and is on display in Belfast.*

SISTER SHIP

Titanic was built alongside its older sister ship, *Olympic*, which was launched on October 20, 1910, and made its maiden voyage to New York on June 14, 1911. Three months later, *Olympic* collided with another ship and had to return to Belfast for repairs, delaying work on *Titanic* by about a month. Both ships were 883 feet long and 92 feet wide. But, at 51,068 tons, *Titanic* weighed around 1,100 tons more, making it the largest ship—and indeed the largest moving manmade object—in the world at the time.

PREPARING THE SITE

A large area was needed to build the ships. The River Lagan next to the shipyard was **dredged** to make it 33 feet deep so the huge ships did not sink into the mud. Three **slipways** were changed into two, one for *Olympic*, one for *Titanic*. A massive steel frame was erected over the workspace, and a powerful floating crane was shipped in from Germany.

January 1912
Installation of all the ship's mechanical components is complete (see pages 20–21).

January 1912
The lifeboats are fitted onto the **davits** on the boat deck (see pages 32–33).

February 1912
The ship is moved to a dry dock so that the hull can be painted and the propellers fitted (see page 19).

April 1912
With the ship now ready, the crew and staff begin to assemble for the maiden journey (see pages 30–31).

Building the ship

Harland & Wolff began assembling *Titanic* in March 1909. The construction of *Olympic* had started four months earlier.

▼ *Titanic (left) was almost identical to Olympic (right), but was slightly heavier.*

HUGE GANTRY

A 220-foot metal framework called a gantry surrounded the two giant ships so that thousands of workmen could fit the hulls together piece by piece. Heavy parts were lifted into place by 17 vast cranes: a stationary revolving one, and 16 movable ones.

▲ *Weighing 200 tons and capable of lifting up to 250 tons, the world's largest floating crane was used during the fitting out of Titanic.*

FROM THE BOTTOM UP

♣ *Titanic* was built from the bottom upward, starting with thick steel beams laid on wooden blocks to form the keel.

♣ 300 curved steel frames were attached like a set of ribs to the keel to define the shape of the hull.

♣ Beams were fitted across the gaps. These would hold up the decks.

♣ Steel plates were riveted to the frame to form the ship's "skin."

The workforce

Many skilled workers were needed to build the giant ship. These included blacksmiths, carpenters, electricians, plumbers, and painters. Of the thousands of men involved in constructing *Titanic*, only a fifth were general workers—the rest were specialists.

PUNISHMENTS

Harland & Wolff was a strict employer. Workers lost money if they broke the rules. They were fined if they took more than their ten-minute morning break or more than half an hour for lunch. There were also fines for arriving late and even for making a cup of tea at the wrong time.

DANGEROUS WORK

The workers toiled from 7.50 a.m. until 5.30 p.m. Monday to Friday, plus Saturday morning. It was a very tough, dangerous job. The men often worked high up on the sides of the ship, dodging the moving cranes. During the build and launch, eight men died and 46 were injured.

▲ *Three million rivets were thumped into place by workers going as fast as they could—they were paid by how many they fitted in each shift.*

▼ *Titanic workers leave the shipyard at the end of the day in 1911. The ship is visible in the background, rising above the buildings.*

Titanic and Olympic each measured just over 880 feet long.

The launch

Titanic was launched on May 31, 1911. Huge crowds around the shipyard cheered as the tall posts holding the giant ship in place were knocked down. The empty metal hull then slid down the ramp and into the water.

WATER SLIDE

The hull weighed about 26,565 tons and sat on wooden blocks. Workers smeared 22 tons of soap, grease, and oil on the 770-foot-long wooden slipway to allow *Titanic* to slide along it and into the water.

▼ *Workers watch from the deck as the giant ship takes to the water for the first time.*

THE FUNNELS

A giant crane hoisted the ship's boilers and funnels into place. Only the first three funnels actually carried fumes away from the boilers. The fourth was a "dummy" put in place to make the ship look more impressive.

It took 62 seconds for the empty hull of *Titanic* to slide down the launch ramp.

STOPPING THE GIANT

At this stage, *Titanic* still had no engines to power it. Massive cables and anchors stopped it from drifting aimlessly in the water. The ship relied on tugs to tow it to the fitting-out basin, where the empty shell was transformed into a palace.

▲ *Titanic's* hull is towed to the fitting-out basin so its engines and interiors can be added.

FITTING OUT

It took ten months to turn the empty hull into a floating hotel.

♣ The engines, boilers, and funnels were fitted.

♣ An army of workers put in the cabins, staterooms, and restaurants.

♣ On February 3, 1912, the ship went into a dry dock to have its propellers fitted and for a final coat of paint.

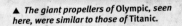

▲ *The giant propellers of* Olympic, *seen here, were similar to those of* Titanic.

◄ *A funnel from Britannic, one of Titanic's sister ships, waits to be lifted into position.*

GIANT ANCHOR

It took massive anchors to hold such a heavy ship. *Titanic's* main anchor weighed 17 tons, and 20 horses were needed to haul it to the shipyard. It was then attached to a 93-ton metal chain that was about 1,000 feet long.

Powering Titanic

Titanic used 750 tons of coal a day. A massive workforce toiled around the clock to keep the furnaces burning, heating the water that produced the steam that powered the engines. All this happened deep down in the ship—the workers who worked and slept on the lower decks probably never even saw the sea.

Titanic ejected around 110 tons of ash into the sea every day.

ENGINES

Titanic had two **reciprocating engines**. Measuring more than 30 feet tall and 62 feet wide, each was bigger than a three-story house and weighed 720 tons. At the time, they were the largest engines of their kind ever built. The exhaust steam they produced fed a large turbine engine set behind them.

▲ *Workers install the blades for the turbine engine on Titanic's sister ship, Britannic.*

TURBINES

The ship's turbine engine was a relatively new invention—the first turbine-powered ship, the *TS King Edward*, had sailed in 1901. A turbine engine had revolving blades and was more efficient than a piston engine. This allowed ships to carry less coal, reducing their weight and giving them more room for passengers, facilities, and cargo.

PROPELLERS

Each engine powered a separate propeller. The two outer propellers had three blades and a diameter of 23 feet, and weighed 38 tons. The slightly smaller 22-ton four-bladed central propeller measured over 16 feet across.

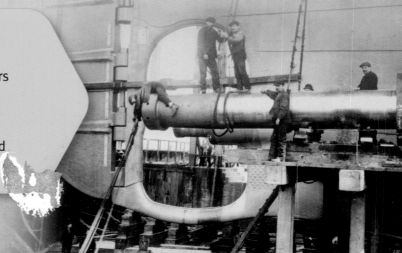

▶ *Workmen prepare to haul one of Titanic's propellers into position.*

ELECTRICITY

Titanic could generate enough electricity to power a small town. Four steam-powered **generators** produced the electricity that passed along 200 miles of cabling to run the ship's electrical equipment. This included bell buttons, potato peelers, heaters, 48 clocks, and no fewer than 10,000 light bulbs. Many of the poorer passengers were unlikely to have had electricity in the homes they had left behind, so the novelty added to *Titanic*'s appeal.

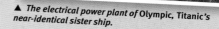

▼ *A long row of boilers provided the steam to drive Titanic's engines.*

▲ *The electrical power plant of* Olympic, Titanic's *near-identical sister ship.*

BOILERS AND FURNACES

Twenty-nine massive water-filled boilers were heated by 159 furnaces and fed steam to the engines. The biggest boilers were 21 feet long and 16 feet in diameter, and needed three furnaces at each end. It took up to 24 hours to heat the water to boiling point so that it turned to steam.

Quality and luxury

Titanic was designed to be the world's most luxurious ocean liner, with large, beautifully decorated cabins and public areas. Harland & Wolff insisted on the highest-quality facilities throughout the first-class sections of the ship, so as to make the journey as comfortable and enjoyable as possible.

SWIM OR STEAM?

First-class passengers could keep fit at the swimming pool, squash court, and gymnasium. Those who preferred to relax instead could head to the richly decorated Turkish baths for a session in the steam room, a refreshing dip in a cool pool, and then a massage.

ROYAL DESIGNS

The decor of the first-class lounge was based on the extravagant design of the French palace of Versailles. The staterooms (first-class cabins) were luxuriously decorated in eleven different historical styles, making them look fit for royal occupation. They featured comforts ranging from deep carpets and proper beds to furniture and electric heaters.

▼ *First-class cabins were equipped with luxurious furniture and fittings.*

About 8000 cigars were loaded on board for the first-class passengers.

Grand staircase

First-class passengers could stroll in style from the boat deck to the first-class dining room four decks below down a grand staircase. It had a wide, curved stairway decorated with gilt-edged railings and carved oak-lined walls.

SPIRALING DOWN

Made up of several sections, the grand staircase was 20 feet wide and spiraled down 56 feet all the way from the first-class entrance on A deck to E deck where the swimming pool and Turkish baths were located. At the foot of each set of stairs stood a bronze cherub.

◄ *The bronze cherub that stood at the foot of the stairway was recovered from the ocean floor in 1987.*

BEAUTIFULLY LIT

A glass dome above the staircase let in plenty of natural light. In the evenings, a huge chandelier set beneath the dome glittered with 50 gold-plated crystal lights. It was all part of the plan to make *Titanic* seem more like a grand hotel than a ship.

▲ *Titanic's grand staircase was almost identical to the one on Olympic, shown here.*

14

First-class staterooms

The first-class rooms and suites were designed to be as good as those in any luxury hotel, with plush carpets, large beds, and sofas. These rooms were located in the middle of the boat where the rocking motion of the sea was felt the least, so passengers were less likely to feel seasick.

FINEST OF ALL

The finest accommodations *Titanic* offered were the two staterooms on A Deck. Each offered a sitting room, two bedrooms, two dressing rooms, a private bathroom, and access to a private 50-foot section of the **promenade** deck where passengers could stroll or sit.

PUBLIC ROOMS

The first-class public rooms were decorated in great style and were large enough to accommodate hundreds of people without them feeling cramped. First-class passenger Dr. Washington Dodge was impressed: "It was hard to realize, when dining in the spacious dining saloon, that one was not in some large and sumptuous hotel."

▼ *The plush furniture of* Titanic's *first-class reading room.*

DOGS WELCOME

Titanic even had kennels to accommodate dogs traveling with first-class passengers. Owners paid £2 (around $100 today) per dog, plus an additional fee to the on-board butchers who provided scraps for the animals to eat. There may have been as many as 12 dogs on the journey. White Star also offered to transport passengers' cats, caged birds, and even monkeys.

◄ *First-class passengers John Jacob Astor and wife Madeleine, walking their dog.*

First-class passengers

The first-class passengers were among the richest people in the USA and Britain at the time. They paid up to £870 (around $45,000 in today's money) for the finest rooms, although a single-**berth** ticket was available for as little as £30 (around $1,300 today).

STAFF ON BOARD

A big team of workers was on hand to serve the needs of the first-class passengers, ranging from stewards, who cleaned the rooms and carried messages to the post room, to restaurant waiters. Many first-class passengers also brought their own staff, such as maids, nurses, and governesses.

WEALTHY TRAVELERS

Among the wealthy travelers journeying home on *Titanic* were:

♣ Isidor Straus, owner of Macy's department store in New York and a member of the US House of Representatives, who was traveling with his wife Ida.

♣ Industrial magnate and businessman Benjamin Guggenheim.

♣ John Jacob Astor, one of the richest men in the world at the time, with an estimated fortune of around $2 billion in today's terms.

♣ Scottish landowner Sir Cosmo Duff-Gordon and his fashion designer wife, Lucy.

◄ *The New York Waldorf-Astoria, one of the world's most luxurious hotels, was part-owned by* Titanic *passenger John Jacob Astor.*

▲ *Isidor Straus (above) and Benjamin Guggenheim (right) both enjoyed the prestige of traveling on* Titanic's *maiden journey.*

There were 325 first-class passengers on board *Titanic* for its maiden voyage.

Second class

Second-class passengers could take afternoon tea in the lounge at 4 p.m. every day.

While not as luxurious or spacious as first class, the second-class facilities on *Titanic* were extremely comfortable and probably as good as the first-class facilities on other liners. The floors may have been tiled rather than carpeted and the beds smaller, but the passengers had access to large, stylish public rooms.

▶ *A replica of one of* Titanic's *second-class cabins, showing its bunk beds and wash basin.*

SECONDS ONLY

Second-class passengers had their own entrance area and staircase as well as an elevator, dining and sitting rooms, a small library, and even a barber shop. They also had a promenade area, although it was on the part of the deck where the hanging lifeboats partly blocked the wide sea views available from the first-class promenade.

▲ *The second-class barber shop of* Titanic's *sister ship,* Olympic.

▲ *Only men were allowed to use* Titanic's *second-class smoking room.*

LOUNGING

The lounge for second-class passengers included a library. This was a smart and stylish room with a beamed ceiling, wooden columns, and six writing tables set on a deep woolen carpet. This room was aimed at women, as men were expected to use the equally plush smoking room, which had oak furniture, a writing desk, and leather-covered settees.

Second-class passengers

Second-class travelers came from the middle section of society and included teachers, businessmen, and clergy. The eight musicians who played on board also had second-class rooms. The typical cost of a second-class ticket was £13 (around $585 today).

▼ Brothers Michel (left, aged 4) and Edmond Navratil (right, aged 2) became famous across the world after the Titanic disaster.

LAST-MINUTE SWITCH

▶ Eva and her mother Esther Hart on board Titanic.

Seven-year-old Eva Hart was due to sail on another ship with her parents when they were switched to *Titanic* at the last moment. She said: "My father was delighted when they offered him a second-class passage in the *Titanic*. The whole world was talking about the *Titanic*."

TITANIC ORPHANS

Among the most poignant *Titanic* stories is that of Michel Navratil from France. Having recently divorced, he was trying to take his children, Michel and Edmond, to the USA without his ex-wife's knowledge. He died in the disaster but the boys were rescued. However, as Michel had booked the tickets under false names, nobody knew who the boys were. Their mother eventually came forward once pictures of the "*Titanic* Orphans" were published in the newspapers.

Titanic had its own newspaper, the Atlantic Daily Bulletin.

Third class

There were just two bathtubs for all of the third-class passengers—one for each sex.

28

Third-class accommodation was known as steerage, because it was located at the **stern** of the ship near its steering mechanism. On *Titanic*, third-class passengers stayed on the lower levels but had access to their own deck space and a large public room. They were also fed well in comparison to third-class passengers on other ships. The typical fare was £7 (around $365 today).

▲ *A replica third-class four-bed cabin on* Titanic *showing the cramped bunks.*

BERTHS NOT DORMS

Most other ships put third-class passengers in large shared rooms called dormitories. But on *Titanic* the majority were given cabins. There were 66 two-berth, 112 four-berth, 37 six-berth, 5 eight-berth, and 2 ten-berth cabins. The single men and women were separated—women in the stern, men in the **bow**. Passengers here were given mattresses, pillows, and blankets, but not sheets.

▼ *The third-class lounge was much plainer than the first and second-class equivalents.*

PUBLIC AREAS

Third-class meals were served at set times in the dining room, where passengers sat on chairs rather than on the benches provided by other liners. They could also gather and socialize in a large general room, in a smoking room (men only), and on the poop deck at the stern—this was behind the smoky funnels, but at least it was in the open air.

Third-class passengers

▲ *Officials conduct medical inspections on immigrants arriving at Ellis Island.*

There were passengers from at least 20 countries in third class, mainly from Europe. Most were emigrants—including families and single people—traveling with all their possessions to start a new life in North America.

CHECK-UP

A doctor inspected third-class passengers before they boarded to check for illness, lice, and other infections. They would be checked again on Ellis Island when they arrived in New York, and those who failed the test would be sent back.

MANY FAMILIES

There were many families in third class, so there were more children here than in other sections—83 were on board. The larger families included John and Annie Sage, migrating to Florida with their nine children, and Frederick and Augusta Goodwin, who took their six children with them, hoping to find work in the USA.

◄ *The entire Goodwin family died in the Titanic disaster.*

LANGUAGE PROBLEMS

Not all third-class passengers spoke English. This made it hard for them to understand the ship's signs and stewards' instructions as they tried to find their rooms in the maze of corridors and decks. Fortunately, an interpreter named Ludwig Müller was among the staff working with third-class passengers, but he wasn't fluent in all the languages spoken.

The toilets in the third-class sections of *Titanic* flushed automatically.

Titanic's workforce

There were 891 crew members on *Titanic*. They included the captain and his officers, stewards who looked after passengers, and the workers below deck who kept the furnaces burning and the engines humming.

▲ *Steward Frederick Dent Ray (1879–1977) was among the 18 stewards who survived the sinking of* Titanic.

THE CREW'S EMPLOYERS

Many of the crew did not actually work for White Star. The two radio operators worked for Marconi—their main job was to handle passengers' messages. The five postal clerks were employed by the US and British mail services. The eight musicians had been booked by an agent to play in the public areas. The first-class restaurant, called À la Carte, operated separately from other food providers on board and employed 66 staff.

▲ *Harold Sydney Bride was the junior wireless radio operator on* Titanic.

SERVING PASSENGERS

The 310 *Titanic* stewards worked long hours to keep passengers happy in all areas of the ship. Some were given a set of cabins to service and often did not stop until the occupants went to bed. They served food and drinks, cleaned rooms, and ran errands for which they hoped to get tips from the passengers.

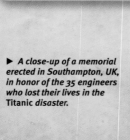

▶ *A close-up of a memorial erected in Southampton, UK, in honor of the 35 engineers who lost their lives in the* Titanic *disaster.*

KEEPING THE SHIP MOVING

A special team worked deep down in the ship, four hours on, eight hours off, to keep the ship running. The team shared a dormitory and included engineers who checked the machinery, trimmers who carried coal from the bunkers to the furnaces, **stokers** who shoveled coal into the furnaces, and greasers who oiled the machines.

The men in charge

Titanic had an experienced crew of officers led by White Star's most revered seaman, Captain Edward John Smith. He took charge of all the firm's maiden voyages. Commanding the *Titanic* was meant to be his last time in charge of a ship before retiring.

OFFICERS

Titanic had eight officers to help run the ship. Each officer had his own special duties:

▲ Captain Edward John Smith

Title	Name	Special duties
Chief Officer	Henry Wilde	*Keep the ship's log (journal)*
Chief Purser	Hugh McElroy	*In charge of the stewards*
First Officer	William Murdoch	*In charge of the cargo and crew*
Second Officer	Charles Lightoller	*In charge of navigation*
Third Officer	Herbert Pitman	*In charge of safety*
Fourth Officer	Joseph Boxall	*Update the ship's charts*
Fifth Officer	Harold Lowe	*Measure air and water temperatures to assess the likelihood of meeting icebergs*
Sixth Officer	James Moody	*In charge of gangways*

▲ First Officer William Murdoch

DANGER SPOTTERS

There were six lookouts, who worked in pairs on two-hour shifts, scanning the sea for dangers such as icebergs. Unfortunately, they weren't equipped with binoculars, which may have helped them to spot the fateful iceberg sooner.

▲ The lookouts tried to spot danger from a platform called the crow's nest, located on the ship's front mast.

▲ Frederick Fleet, the 24-year-old lookout who spotted the iceberg first.

Some passengers traveled on the *Titanic* because of Smith's reputation as a captain.

22

Lifeboats and lifebelts

Today we find it hard to understand why *Titanic* had fewer lifeboat places than there were people on board, but this was normal practice for 1912. There were actually more lifeboats than required by the laws of the time, and *Titanic* was regarded as one of the safest ships on the water.

MORE THAN NEEDED

The ship also carried four "Collapsibles"—wooden boats with canvas sides that were stored on the boat deck. These had room for 47 people. With the other lifeboats, that made a total of 1,178 places, which was more than the legal requirement. But *Titanic* had around 2,200 people on board. However, 6,560 lifejackets were available.

◄ *Lifeboats were stored on the boat deck of* Titanic *and* Olympic *(shown here).*

NUMBERS

Titanic's first designer, Alexander Carlisle, made plans for the ship to have 40 lifeboats— quite a large number. As it turned out, *Titanic* set sail with just 16 lifeboats: 14 with room for 65 people and two smaller craft called cutters that could carry 40 people each. Carlisle retired from Harland & Wolff in 1910, passing the job of head designer on to Thomas Andrews.

UNSINKABLE?

Titanic was widely thought to be extremely safe because of its watertight compartments. Even if the ship did hit something, experts believed it would sink so slowly that there would be plenty of time for help to arrive. In fact, many thought the lifeboats would come in useful only if *Titanic* met a less fortunate ship that was in trouble.

▲ *Designers in the Harland & Wolff drafting office carefully planned every aspect of* Titanic's *design, including the number of lifeboats.*

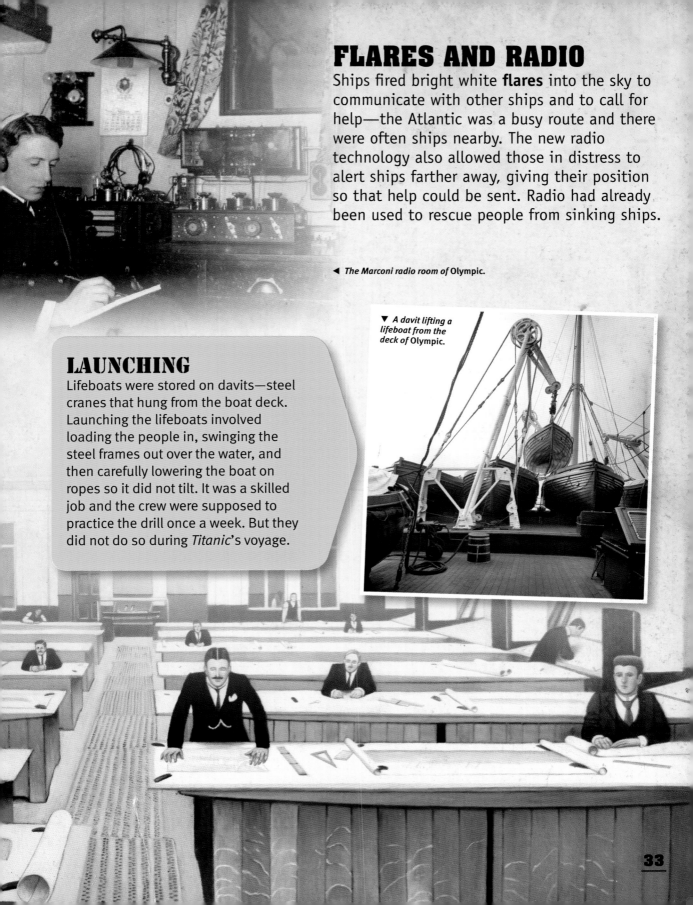

FLARES AND RADIO

Ships fired bright white **flares** into the sky to communicate with other ships and to call for help—the Atlantic was a busy route and there were often ships nearby. The new radio technology also allowed those in distress to alert ships farther away, giving their position so that help could be sent. Radio had already been used to rescue people from sinking ships.

◀ *The Marconi radio room of* Olympic.

LAUNCHING

Lifeboats were stored on davits—steel cranes that hung from the boat deck. Launching the lifeboats involved loading the people in, swinging the steel frames out over the water, and then carefully lowering the boat on ropes so it did not tilt. It was a skilled job and the crew were supposed to practice the drill once a week. But they did not do so during *Titanic*'s voyage.

▼ *A davit lifting a lifeboat from the deck of* Olympic.

The journey

White Star offered a sailing across the Atlantic every Wednesday, but *Titanic*'s journey would be a little different. It was the maiden voyage of the company's newest, largest, and most prestigious ship. White Star's chief Bruce Ismay was on board to mark the occasion and he was eager to boast about arriving early in New York, ahead of the usual time.

Over 100,000 people turned up to see *Titanic*'s launch.

▶ *Henry Wilde had also held the role of chief officer on* Olympic *and was thought of as a future captain of* Titanic.

OFFICERS CHANGED

A few days before *Titanic* sailed, White Star changed the top officers. The company brought in Henry Wilde from *Olympic* as chief officer. This meant Officer William Murdoch was moved down to the position of first officer, and Lightoller to second officer. The decision changed their responsibilities and reduced their pay. They were not very happy about this.

MAIDEN VOYAGES

Maiden voyages were good for publicity, as newspapers liked to cover the stories and mention famous passengers on board and features of the new ship. For White Star, *Titanic* was its latest and most impressive ship, and it was expecting positive media coverage.

KEY EVENTS

April 2, 1912
After a brief sea trial, *Titanic* leaves Belfast for Southampton to pick up passengers (see page 36).

April 4, 1912
Captain Smith reshuffles the senior crew to bring in Henry Wilde from *Olympic* as chief officer (see above).

April 6, 1912
The cancellation of some liner sailings sees passengers transferred to *Titanic* (see page 36).

April 9, 1912
The ship's cargo, including 3,000 bags of mail, is loaded on board (see page 41).

AHEAD OF TIME

Some historians believe that Bruce Ismay was eager for *Titanic* to beat the journey time of its sister ship *Olympic*. He is known to have discussed the speed of travel with both the captain and passengers during the voyage, and even to have said that it might dock on Tuesday night, not Wednesday morning as had originally been planned.

◀ *Bruce Ismay, the chairman of White Star.*

▶ *Charlotte Collyer and her daughter, Marjorie, survived the sinking, but her husband Harvey died.*

PASSENGER REACTIONS

Everyone seemed to be thrilled to be joining the maiden voyage of such a famous ship.

♣ Charlotte Collyer, emigrating with her husband and daughter, wrote: "*Titanic* was wonderful, far more splendid and huge than I had dreamed of. The other crafts in the harbour were like cockle shells beside her."

♣ "This ship is like a palace," wrote Lawrence Beesley to his daughter. "My cabin is ripping (good), hot and cold water and a very comfy looking bed and plenty of room."

April 10, 1912

As *Titanic* pulls away from the quay, it nearly strikes another ship (see page 37).

April 10, 1912

Titanic completes the first part of its journey, arriving at Cherbourg, France (see page 40).

April 11, 1912

Titanic stops briefly at Queenstown, Ireland, to collect more mail and passengers (see page 40).

April 14, 1912

At 5:50 p.m., the ship changes course at the "Corner" to head for New York, as planned (see pages 44–45).

Titanic departs

Titanic set off from Southampton at midday on April 10, 1912, with **958** passengers on board. Some people had been transferred to the ship at the last moment after other voyages had been canceled because of coal shortages. The passengers were excited to be traveling on the biggest ship in the world.

A BUSY WEEK

Titanic had arrived in Southampton the previous week following a brief test voyage known as a sea trial. Finishing touches continued to be made to the ship until the last minute. After the ship was loaded with coal, the cleaners struggled to clear the dust that had spread up into the ship. Meanwhile, stewards placed lots of vases of flowers in the public areas, hoping that their perfume would mask the smell of fresh paint.

Thirteen couples on board *Titanic* were celebrating their honeymoons.

▶ Titanic *sets off on its sea trial off the coast of Belfast on April 2.*

WHITE STAR LINE

BOARDING PASS

PERMISSION GRANTED TO COME ABOARD
WHITE STAR LINE'S
R.M.S.
TITANIC

ISMAY, IMRIE & CO.,
34, LEADENHALL STREET, LONDON,
AND
10, WATER STREET, LIVERPOOL.

WELCOME ABOARD

The different classes of passenger were each greeted differently:

♣ First-class travelers were welcomed by officers as they stepped onto B or D deck. The men were given a flower for their buttonhole.

♣ Second-class travelers came down a gangway on C deck. They were allowed to tour the first-class area, including its gymnasium—which they were not allowed to visit during the voyage.

♣ Third-class travelers arrived on E deck, lower down, for a quick medical inspection—anybody carrying a disease would not be allowed into the USA. They then headed down into the depths of the ship to find their cabins.

◀ *Passengers wait to board* Titanic *at Southampton.*

TOO LATE TO JOIN

The last of the crew was hired just days before the voyage. Two stokers who were late arriving at the quayside ran up, panting, with their kit bags over their shoulders. They shouted to be allowed on board, but officer James Moody angrily waved them away and raised the gangway. The men missed the voyage.

◀ *Sixth Officer James Moody.*

THAT WAS CLOSE!

As *Titanic* eased from the quayside, cables holding a ship called the *New York* snapped and the ship swung out toward the giant liner. Passengers waving from the decks were alarmed as the two ships drifted to within 3 feet of each other. The incident delayed *Titanic*'s departure by an hour.

Taking the air

▲ *Passengers walk on the boat deck of* Titanic *between the funnels and lifeboats.*

Promenading was a popular pastime of the age. Many British seaside towns had areas where people could walk and chat or relax in deckchairs. *Titanic* offered them the chance to do the same at sea. In fact, deck A, where first-class passengers went to socialize in the open air, was also known as the promenade deck.

SITTING ROOM

Anyone who chose not to promenade could sit on a deckchair protected from the wind and cold air by a rug decorated with the White Star insignia. A chair could be hired for the whole voyage for 4 shillings (around $11 in today's money).

SOCIAL DIVISIONS

First-class passengers were allocated the entire length of deck A, spanning 545 feet, for their promenades. The main second-class promenade was, fittingly, underneath this on deck B and was just 82 feet long. Second-class passengers could also take a sneaky look at the two private sections next to the top-priced first-class staterooms.

White Star fitted extra windows on the boat deck to keep out sea spray.

THIRD CLASS

Third-class passengers who were eager to get into the open air had two choices. The single men in cabins near the front of the ship could use part of the forward well deck, which was also used by the "Black Gang"—the crew who shoveled coal into the furnaces. The others, mainly women and families, had access to an area on the poop deck. This was in the stern section, behind the funnels, so the air could be full of smoke and ash if the wind was blowing in the wrong direction.

▲ *The boat deck provided an outdoor playground for children.*

▼ *Deckchairs lined up on the promenade deck of* Olympic, *which was similar to the one on* Titanic.

DECK GAMES

Passengers played deck games such as quoits, in which players throw rope rings at a target, and shuffleboard, where wooden handles are used to push weights across the wooden planks to try to hit a target. Promenades were also places where children could run around and relax.

Stop-offs

Titanic did not sail west right away. Instead, it crossed the English Channel to the French **port** of Cherbourg, then back to Queenstown (now Cobh) in Ireland, before heading across the Atlantic. At each stop-off, a few people disembarked while many more climbed aboard.

LATE ARRIVAL

First-class passengers were annoyed that *Titanic* arrived an hour late (because of the incident with the *New York*), especially since these rich, powerful people were not used to waiting. They included the American millionaire, John Jacob Astor, who was returning from his honeymoon with his young bride.

TWO TENDERS

Cherbourg harbor was too shallow to take *Titanic*, so the 274 passengers booked on the voyage were ferried out on two large boats known as **tenders**. The Laroche family joined the ship here. Traveling second class, Joseph and Juliette Laroche had two daughters and another child on the way. They were returning to Haiti, where Joseph was born.

◀ *Joseph Laroche died in the* Titanic *disaster, but his family survived.*

Atlantic Ocean

BELFAST ●

Queenstown ●   ● Southampton

Cherbourg ●

Atlantic Ocean

NEW YORK
×

▲ *Map showing* Titanic's *route. The "X" marks the spot where it sank.*

ON TO IRELAND

After leaving Cherbourg, *Titanic* sailed overnight to Ireland. Again, the port (Queenstown, now called Cobh) was too shallow for the giant ship, so tenders ferried the passengers aboard. A number of Irish lace sellers also boarded the ship and sold their wares to passengers before returning to shore. They were joined by a stoker called John Coffey who decided to "jump ship" and sneaked onto the tender, where he hid among the sacks of mail until it reached land.

◀ Titanic *in Queenstown harbor.*

A further 1,385 bags of mail were loaded while the ship was at Queenstown.

Titanic's cargo

As well as passengers, *Titanic* also transported cargo and mail across the Atlantic. Both were a major source of income for White Star, and added weight (about 900 tons) to the ship, making it more stable.

TITANIC POST

Titanic was carrying more than 3,000 bags of mail. The "RMS" in "*RMS Titanic*" stands for "Royal Mail Steamer," and showed that the ship's owners had a contract to carry mail to and from Britain. Landing this contract in 1876 had played a big part in White Star's early success. The mail was stored below the post room on G Deck.

▼ *A modern recreation of the 1912 Renault CB Coupe de Ville bought by William Carter during his European vacation.*

ALL KINDS OF CARGO

Titanic's cargo included thousands of items that were part of everyday life, such as straw hats, perfumes, and books. Also lifted into the hold were:

♣ 76 boxes of dragon's blood—a red-colored resin used in varnishes and medicines.

♣ 12 cases of ostrich feathers (for fashionable hats).

♣ A Renault car belonging to first-class passenger William Carter.

♣ Two grandfather clocks.

♣ 79 goats' skins (probably to be made into gloves).

♣ An Edison gramophone—the latest way to play music at the time.

FL 3698

FATHER BROWNE

A student priest named Frank Browne left at Queenstown. He was an avid amateur photographer, and took the only surviving pictures on board *Titanic* during its journey. He wanted to continue to New York, but when he sent a message to his boss asking to stay on, he was told to "get off that ship."

Titanic also carried 15 cases of rabbit hair and one barrel of earth.

Radio communications

28

Titanic carried the latest communication equipment—radio—not primarily for safety reasons, but to receive news from around the world and for passengers to send "Marconigrams" to friends. *Titanic* was among the first liners to have radio technology on board (see page 7).

(see page 7)

RADIO ROOMS

The three radio rooms were on the boat deck tucked in between the first and second funnels. There was an office where messages were handed in, a room for the transmitter (which made such a loud noise that the walls had to be soundproofed), and a cabin for the two staff who ran the service.

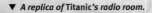
▼ *A replica of* Titanic's *radio room.*

WEAK OR STRONG

The radio men tapped out messages using the dots and dashes of **Morse code**, and received messages through headphones, quickly translating them back into words. The farther the ship was from a receiver, the weaker the signal became. On Sunday, April 14, *Titanic* was transmitting 800 miles to Cape Race, Newfoundland. The signal was hard to hear, and transmissions from nearer ships sometimes drowned out the sound. This was to prove important before the sinking.

▶ Titanic's *radio antenna was strung between its two masts.*

Antenna

RADIO STAFF

The two radio operators were Jack Phillips and Harold Bride. Officially employed by radio company Marconi, they had their working hours arranged so that there was someone at their post 24 hours a day. Their main job was to send and receive messages called "Marconigrams" for *Titanic* passengers. Marconigrams cost 12 shillings, 6 pence, for the first ten words and 9 pence for every word after that. A typical message would cost $65 at today's prices.

▶ *Jack George Phillips celebrated his 25th birthday on board* Titanic.

ICE WARNINGS

If ships saw ice—one of the dangers on the journey—they would send out warnings to other ships. When the Marconi staff received warnings, they would take them to their ship's officers, who would mark the danger on a map and decide whether it was serious enough to steer away from. But there was no system to ensure these warnings reached the officers.

LONG NIGHT

Both radio operators were tired on Sunday, having worked till 5 a.m. to fix equipment that had broken down the night before. By then, a huge number of messages had piled up and the operators struggled all day to catch up. This may explain why some ice warnings did not reach the bridge.

Across the Atlantic

The only way to cross the Atlantic at this time was by ship. At any one time, there might be 100 ships making the 3,100-mile journey between Europe and North America. Ships usually followed the same routes, called shipping lanes. There were no islands along most of these routes, so the journey had to be done in one step.

DISTANCE TRAVELED

At midday each day, officers put up notices to inform passengers how far *Titanic* had traveled. Passengers loved this information—some even placed bets on what the next day's figure would be. The unit used to measure the distance was the nautical mile, which equals 1.15 land miles.

The figures were:

- ⚙ Friday, April 12: 484 nautical miles
- ⚙ Saturday, April 13: 519 nautical miles
- ⚙ Sunday, April 14: 546 nautical miles

FIXING POSITION

Officers could calculate their location by measuring the height of the Sun at dawn, noon, and dusk. Between these, they estimated their position by "dead reckoning"—using information on how fast the ship was traveling, the ship's course (whether it had made any turns), and the current (movement of the sea) to plot *Titanic*'s location on the map.

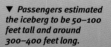

▼ *Passengers estimated the iceberg to be 50–100 feet tall and around 300–400 feet long.*

THE CORNER

Ships making their way across the Atlantic made a final turn on the route to line themselves up for New York. This was known as the "Corner." *Titanic* made this turn without any problems at 5:50 p.m. on Sunday, April 14.

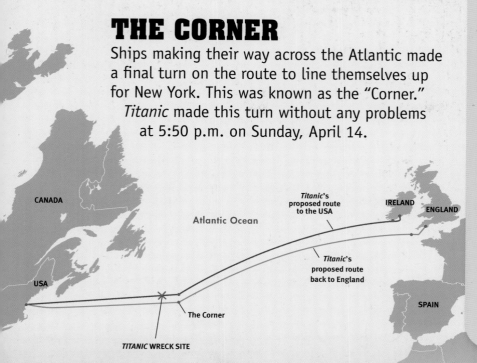

CANADA

Atlantic Ocean

Titanic's proposed route to the USA

IRELAND

ENGLAND

USA

Titanic's proposed route back to England

SPAIN

The Corner

TITANIC WRECK SITE

▲ *Map showing the Corner, where* Titanic *turned for New York shortly before disaster struck.*

ICEBERGS

Icebergs are huge chunks of ice that fall, or "calve," off glaciers in the Arctic. The ice has compacted over thousands of years and is as hard as iron. Only a small part of the iceberg is visible—most is hidden underwater. Nearly all the icebergs melt near the Arctic, but every year, about 400 float south into the Atlantic. The route the icebergs take is known as "Iceberg Alley."

AVOIDING ICEBERGS

The biggest danger to a transatlantic liner was hitting another ship, a submerged rock, or an iceberg. The main ways to avoid icebergs were:

☘ To sail south of Iceberg Alley.

☘ If the ship became stuck in an ice field, to slow down and even come to a complete stop at night.

☘ To listen for radio warnings from other ships, giving officers the opportunity to change course.

☘ To check the sea and air temperatures regularly and to take the necessary action if there was a drop.

☘ To station lookouts to watch for ice from the crow's nest—a platform on a mast above the bridge. They were trained to look for reflected moonlight, dark shapes, and the foam from waves breaking on the iceberg. If they saw anything, they rang the ship's bell and used a telephone to call the bridge.

On-board entertainment

Titanic was a busy ship and offered plenty of activities for first-class passengers in particular. They could read in the library, write and send postcards, listen to music, attend church services, take exercise on deck or in the gymnasium, play games indoors or out on deck...or just wander the stairs and corridors to explore the vast floating hotel.

SWIMMING AND SQUASH

The swimming pool was 36 feet long and filled with sea water that was heated to make it more comfortable to bathe in. Passengers could also try out the recently invented game of squash on *Titanic*'s own squash court, where they could even hire an instructor to teach them how to play.

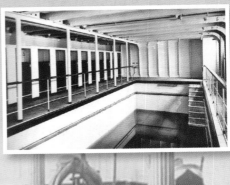

▼ Olympic *and* Titanic *were the first ships to have swimming pools on board.*

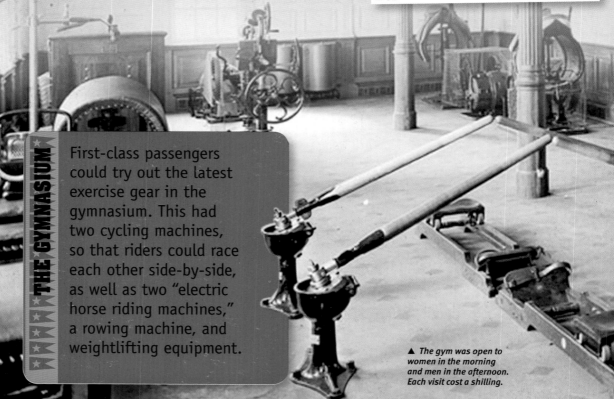

THE GYMNASIUM

First-class passengers could try out the latest exercise gear in the gymnasium. This had two cycling machines, so that riders could race each other side-by-side, as well as two "electric horse riding machines," a rowing machine, and weightlifting equipment.

▲ *The gym was open to women in the morning and men in the afternoon. Each visit cost a shilling.*

Lights in third-class public areas were turned out at 10 p.m. to encourage people to go to bed.

46

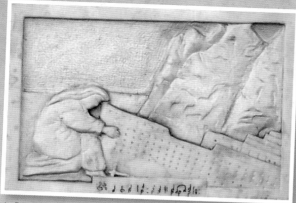

▲ *Detail of a memorial, in Southampton, UK, dedicated to the Titanic musicians. All of the musicians died in the disaster.*

MUSIC ON TITANIC

The eight professional musicians on board *Titanic* formed two bands, a trio and a quintet. The quintet was particularly busy, playing daily in the first and second-class sections. They performed for two hours from 10 a.m., another two hours at 4 p.m., then again after dinner from 8 p.m. to 10:15 p.m. The trio played only in the first-class restaurant. The musicians stayed in second-class accommodation with an extra cabin to store their instruments.

SMOKING ROOMS

There were three smoking rooms, one for each class. Only men could use them, as it was not thought "proper" for women to smoke in public at the time. The first-class room had stained-glass windows and wooden paneling and a real fireplace to look like a gentleman's club. The large, ornately decorated second-class smoking room was lit by 75 ceiling lights. The third-class equivalent was smaller but still very spacious, with green leather tabletops.

GAMES

Board and card games were provided for first and second-class passengers to play inside, as well as deck games outside. Third-class travelers, on the other hand, had to find ways to entertain themselves. Second-class passenger Lawrence Beesley watched the third-class passengers "enjoying every minute of the time: a most uproarious skipping game...was a great favorite."

Food on board

The food on *Titanic* was as good as that served in the top restaurants of the day. Even the third-class menu was far superior to that on other liners. Three meals per day were included in the ticket price. *Titanic* carried a mountain of provisions with staff serving up to 7,000 meals every day.

FIRST-CLASS FOOD

A bugler played to announce the first-class meals, which in the evening could be an eleven-course marathon (as it was on the Sunday night when the ship sank). Both men and women dressed in their best clothes for this special event, held in a dining room with space for 550 people. Fine food was served at tables adorned with white tablecloths, flowers, and baskets of fresh fruit. Musicians played while the diners chatted and ate.

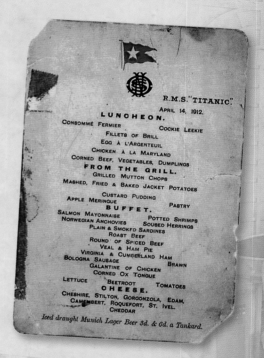

▶ *A rare surviving copy of the final first-class lunch menu features a wide range of main dishes, desserts, and cheeses.*

PLATE CLASSES

First-class diners ate from fine china plates, sometimes decorated with gold leaf. The plates in second class were blue and white, while third-class crockery carried the White Star logo, possibly to discourage people from stealing a cup or plate as a souvenir.

▲ *A replica* Titanic *second-class plate bearing the White Star logo.*

OTHER CHOICES

First-class passengers had the choice of eating in the upmarket À la Carte restaurant or the Café Parisien. Here, they had to pay extra for their food—it cost at least 12 shillings and 6 pence to dine in the restaurant (around $33 in today's money), so a meal for five could cost more than the cheapest third-class fare. But diners could eat at any time of the day and sit with whomever they liked. In the dining rooms, passengers sat on the same seat for every meal with the same neighbors, which didn't suit everyone.

◄ *The second-class dining room of Olympic.*

SECOND AND THIRD CLASS

Second-class meals were served in two separate sittings. The food was not as lavish as in first class, but included roast meats, chicken curry, and spaghetti dishes. In the third-class kitchen, the busy chefs cooked up large quantities of food. A typical meal would consist of soup, fresh bread, roast beef, and dessert. The dining room was divided by a wall to separate the single men from the families and women.

▲ *Café Parisien was decorated to look like a French sidewalk café.*

TITANIC MEALS

There were five kitchens on board operated by 62 members of staff. The ship carried huge amounts of provisions, including:

- 40,000 eggs • 900 pounds of grapes
- 1,500 gallons of fresh milk • 16,000 lemons
- 40 tons of potatoes • 440 gallons of ice cream
- 57,600 pieces of crockery
- 29,000 items of glassware
- 44,000 pieces of cutlery

Life for the crew

The crew's job was to keep everything running smoothly, from maintaining the engines that powered the ship to making sure the bed sheets were changed and the cabin heaters were working. They also had to stay out of the way—the crew had separate staircases so they didn't bump into passengers.

▲ *Chief Purser McElroy (left) with Captain Smith aboard* Titanic.

PASSENGER CONTACT

The officer that the first-class passengers met most often was the chief purser, Hugh McElroy. He was in charge of the ship's finances. His roles included collecting the receipts from the bars and Marconi room, keeping the jewelry of the first-class passengers secure in a large safe, and handing out those necklaces and earrings they wanted to wear for the evening meal. McElroy also dined with the first-class passengers. He did not survive the voyage.

THE BLACK GANG

Mostly hidden away from the passengers was the "Black Gang"—so called because these crew members often became covered in dust from shoveling coal to keep the massive furnaces burning. It was a job that required skill as well as strength. For example, the trimmers who wheeled the coal to the furnaces got their name from the fact that they had to keep the ship "in trim"—balanced so it was stable—which meant they could not empty one side of the ship and leave the other full.

Only about 50 of the crew were actually seamen who knew how to sail the ship.

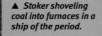

▲ *Stoker shoveling coal into furnaces in a ship of the period.*

Life for the stewards

There were 51 stewards serving the third-class passengers and 76 in second class. But most stewards preferred to be among the 225 attending to first-class needs, as they were more likely to get a tip from grateful passengers at the end of the journey.

LATE NIGHTS, EARLY STARTS

Stewards worked very long hours. Many had to be on call for as long as the passengers were awake. The first-class reading and writing room stayed open until 11:30 p.m., and the smoking room until midnight. Some stewards stayed on duty well into the night, making sure passengers had everything they wanted. They then had to be up early the next day.

HARD WORK

Violet Jessop, a stewardess on *Titanic*, described her days as being filled with "bell answering, slop emptying, floor washing, bed making, tea carrying, or the trundling of baggage." She complained that stewards rarely had time to sit and eat: "The very food stewards eat was always taken standing in any available corner of a greasy pantry, amid steamy smells... eaten in the quickest possible time."

◀ *Stewardess Violet Jessop was the only crew member to survive the sinking of both* Titanic *and, in 1916, its sister ship,* Britannic, *as well as a previous accident in 1911 involving* Olympic.

UNUSUAL JOBS

Several members of the crew had unusual jobs. They included Percy Fletcher, the bugler who announced mealtimes, the man who ran the gym, Thomas McCauley, and the squash instructor, Fred Wright. Some stewards were also employed to walk the passengers' dogs along the deck.

Each steward was given a set of cabins to look after and got to know the passengers well.

34 ▶ The sinking

Even after *Titanic* hit the iceberg, very few people thought it would sink. Its passengers, crew, and designer expected the great ship to stay afloat and, even if it could not continue its journey, that help would arrive. But *Titanic* was mortally wounded.

FIRST TO KNOW

With his detailed knowledge of the ship, designer Thomas Andrews became a key figure after *Titanic* struck the iceberg. He hurried below deck to check on the rising water and tried to reassure passengers. He was alarmed at 12:10 a.m. to see that three of the watertight compartments were flooded. Fifteen minutes later he realized *Titanic* was sinking fast. He also knew there weren't enough lifeboat places for those on board. Andrews stayed on board as the ship went down.

▲ *Andrews threw deckchairs, such as this one, overboard to act as life rafts for people in the water.*

THE BAND PLAYED ON

At 12:15 a.m., some of *Titanic*'s musicians made their way upstairs and began playing cheerful music. It seems they wanted to help keep people calm. However, hearing them play may have made some passengers assume there was no great danger, delaying their decision to take action. Sadly, the band was washed into the sea with the ship.

KEY EVENTS

April 14, 1912

11:40 p.m.: Lookouts spot the iceberg, which the ship strikes about 30 seconds later (see page 54).

April 14, 1912

11:50 p.m.: Mail clerks try to rescue mail bags as the front of the ship starts to flood (see page 55).

April 15, 1912

12:15 a.m.: The band starts playing and passengers are told to put on lifejackets (see above and page 57).

April 15, 1912

12:25 a.m.: Thomas Andrews realizes the ship is sinking—Captain Smith orders its evacuation (see page 56).

COMING BACK

As the lifeboats drifted in the sea, horrified survivors heard the screams of people struggling in the freezing water. Many discussed whether they should go back, but some were afraid the lifeboats would become swamped by too many people climbing aboard. In the end, just two boats went back, by which time there were only a few people alive in the icy waves.

OVERCONFIDENCE

When Lucy Duff-Gordon woke up her husband to tell him the ship was in danger, he said, "Don't be so ridiculous. Even if we have grazed an iceberg it can't do any serious damage with all these watertight compartments. The worst that can happen is that it will slow us down. Go back to bed and don't worry." It was a typical view of many passengers and crew on board.

▲ Titanic *survivors row their lifeboats away from the sinking ship.*

▶ *The fashion designer Lady Duff-Gordon escaped* Titanic *in Lifeboat 1.*

April 15, 1912
12:27 a.m.: *Titanic* sends the first of many distress calls by radio, asking for help (see page 56).

April 15, 1912
12:45 a.m.: Officers fire flares into the sky, trying to attract nearby ships (see page 56).

April 15, 1912
12:45 a.m.: The lifeboats begin to be launched, one at a time, many far from full (see pages 58–61).

April 15, 1912
2:17 a.m.: The ship breaks in two and sinks—those left behind go down with ship (see pages 62–65).

35 Iceberg ahead!

At 11:40 p.m. on Sunday, April 14, lookout Frederick Fleet rang *Titanic*'s warning bell and yelled into the crow's nest telephone: "Iceberg right ahead!" First Officer Murdoch ordered the ship to turn left—but it was too late. Just half a minute later, *Titanic*'s right (starboard) side crashed into the iceberg.

SILENCE

Following the impact, First Officer Murdoch ordered the closing of the watertight doors. The ship's engines stopped for the first time in the voyage and *Titanic* sat in silence. However, the furnaces were still burning and making steam, which had to be released before the pressure caused an explosion. It was let out through the funnel, making a piercing shriek.

◄ *Titanic approaches the iceberg that would rip several large holes in its hull beneath the waterline.*

▲ *The iceberg that may have sank* Titanic, *photographed by a passing ship the following morning.*

HARD TO SPOT

Why didn't the lookouts spot the iceberg sooner?

- ❧ It was a dark, moonless night.

- ❧ The sea was calm, so no waves broke against the iceberg.

- ❧ The lookouts didn't have binoculars.

Why did Titanic flood?

Titanic flooded because six of its watertight compartments had been punctured and were filling with water. The water ran over the unsealed tops of the **bulkheads** into the compartments behind, and its weight tipped the ship, causing more overflowing.

▼ As more water flooded into Titanic following the collision, the bow of the ship began to be dragged underwater.

Sea level

Bulkhead (15 in total)

Rising water level

The iceberg caused six gashes in the hull.

MAILROOM FILLING UP

The screech of the escaping steam aside, most people on board *Titanic* were unconcerned by the ship coming to a halt. But below deck, stokers desperately scrambled up ladders to escape the water rushing in through gaps in the hull. At about 11:50 p.m., mailroom staff emerged wet to the knees, dragging bags of mail with them as their storeroom flooded. It was at this point that some of the crew became alarmed. They realized water was entering the front of the ship and rising through the decks. Soon, the first-class baggage room and the squash court were flooded, and the crew heard hissing noises as air from the hold was pushed out by the incoming sea water.

Titanic had been designed to stay afloat if only four of its compartments flooded.

Disbelief and danger

Some passengers slept through the crash. Others were alarmed by the grating sound the iceberg made as it scraped along the side of the ship. A few even saw the mountain of ice glide past their window. Several passengers rushed onto the decks and kicked around chunks of ice that the collision had thrown on board. Few were seriously worried. After all, everyone believed *Titanic* was the safest ship in the world.

▼ Beesley (right), shown here in the gym, survived the disaster.

JOKES

Lawrence Beesley was chatting with some men in the second-class smoking room when the iceberg struck. Like most passengers, they were not worried. "I expect the iceberg has scratched off some of her new paint," said one, "and the captain doesn't like to go on until she is painted up again." Everyone laughed, and someone jokingly pointed to his glass and asked for some ice from the chunks on the deck.

IN DISTRESS

At 12:25 a.m., Thomas Andrews informed Captain Smith that five of the watertight compartments were flooded. *Titanic* was sinking! The captain instructed the radio operators to send out a message asking any nearby ships for help, and ordered the evacuation of the ship. Twenty minutes later, officers fired white distress flares into the dark sky. The watching passengers suddenly realized they were in grave danger.

Officers could judge the ship's increasing tilt using an instrument called an inclinometer.

56

► *Survivor Edith Rosenbaum carrying a pig-shaped music box which she used to calm children in Lifeboat 11.*

LIFEJACKETS

There were no loudspeakers on *Titanic*. Stewards frantically knocked on cabin doors and told passengers to put on their lifejackets and come to the boat deck to board the lifeboats. The jackets were stored in the cabins and were tricky to tie in place. Some passengers hurriedly threw them on over their nightclothes. Others struggled to stretch warm coats on top of them.

▲ *Titanic lifejackets were made of cork, which floats easily, covered in canvas.*

FUSS OR DANGER?

Edith Rosenbaum in first class complained to her steward, Robert Wareham, about all the fuss. He replied: "It's a rule of the Board of Trade that...in the threat of danger lifebelts will be donned by the passengers. Not that I think this ship can sink. She's an unsinkable ship, everybody knows that." Other stewards and passengers were saying the same: even if *Titanic* was damaged, it would stay afloat.

Loading the lifeboats

There were 16 boats hanging on frames on either side of the ship. Passengers lined up to get on them before officers ordered them to be lowered 70 feet into the dark, ice-cold sea.

PLUG THAT HOLE!

When Lifeboat 7 reached the sea, it started filling with water because the plughole that let out rainwater on deck had not been plugged. The occupants, including silent film actress Dorothy Gibson, stuffed clothing into the hole to prevent more water gushing in.

LIFEBOAT MAYHEM

The occupants of Lifeboat 13 used oars to push their boat away from the side of the ship. But it drifted to the spot where Lifeboat 15 was being lowered onto. Everyone shouted frantically, which stopped the crew from dropping the second boat on top of the first.

◀ *Lifeboat 15 almost lands on top of Lifeboat 13.*

ROW AWAY

Officers made sure there were crewmen in each lifeboat who knew how to sail it. As each boat hit the water, one steered while others picked up the oars and began to row. They were anxious to pull away from *Titanic* because they feared being sucked down with it if it sank.

▼ *Passengers remain on deck as the lifeboats row away from the ship.*

Launched half-full

Not only did *Titanic* not have enough lifeboat places for everyone on board, many of the boats were launched nowhere near full.

DELAYS ❄❄❄

Such was *Titanic*'s reputation that it took people a long time to realize the ship was sinking very quickly. It was also a freezing night, so many passengers preferred to stay inside rather than brave the icy air on deck to see what was happening for themselves.

▼ *Titanic* officers Charles Lightoller (left) and Herbert Pitman after the sinking.

CLASS DIFFERENCES

The first-class accommodation was near the top of the ship, where the lifeboats were kept, so these passengers were the first to reach them. Third-class passengers had to make their way along a maze of corridors and stairways, and many did not read English well enough to follow the instructions and signs.

PORT VS STARBOARD

On the port side, Officer Lightoller put only women and children in the boats. But on the starboard side, Officer Murdoch also allowed men to climb in if there was room. Each lifeboat had 65 seats. These were the numbers on board each lifeboat:

Port side (Lightoller)	Number on board	Starboard side (Murdoch)	Number on board
Lifeboat 8	25	Lifeboat 7	28
Lifeboat 6	26	Lifeboat 5	41
Lifeboat 14	60	Lifeboat 3	32
Lifeboat 16	52	Lifeboat 1	12
Lifeboat 12	42	Lifeboat 9	56
Lifeboat 2	17	Lifeboat 11	70
Lifeboat 4	42	Lifeboat 13	64
Lifeboat 10	57	Lifeboat 15	70
Total	321	**Total**	373

A lifeboat drill planned for the morning of the disaster was canceled at the last moment.

Last chance

The last four lifeboats on the boat deck were foldaway vessels called collapsibles. Known as boats A, B, C, and D, they had wooden hulls and canvas sides, which meant they weren't as sturdy as normal lifeboats.

TWO LAUNCHED

In the icy cold conditions and with *Titanic* sinking rapidly, the crew struggled with the tricky job of slotting in iron supports to stretch the fabric tight so the collapsibles could be loaded into the davits, which would then lower them into the sea. Only two were launched—C and D.

▲ *The survivors in Collapsible D row themselves to safety.*

LIFE-SAVING JUMP!

Third-class passenger Sahid Nackid handed his baby daughter to his wife in Collapsible C. But an officer stopped him from joining her. As the boat was being lowered, he jumped over the deck rails, landing face down in the bottom of the lifeboat. The women hid him under their skirts to prevent him from being spotted.

PULLED OUT OF THE OCEAN

First-class passenger Frederick Hoyt waved goodbye to his wife Jane as she was lowered into Collapsible D. Captain Smith told him he would have to jump to save himself and added, "you had better do it soon." Hoyt threw off his overcoat and leapt into the dark water. The occupants of the collapsible hauled him in and as he lay shivering on the bottom of the craft, his distressed wife realized he was saved after all.

▲ *Collapsible B is recovered after the disaster.*

OVERTURNED

The unlaunched Collapsibles A and B were swept into the sea as *Titanic* sank under the water. Collapsible B tipped over, and people in the sea climbed onto the upturned hull. The lucky ones were rescued by other boats, having clung on all night, while others slipped beneath the waves.

FUNNEL DANGER

Washed overboard, first-class passenger Richard Norris Williams spotted his father Charles and swam toward him. They were just a few meters apart when one of *Titanic*'s giant funnels broke off and crashed into the water. It killed Charles outright and sent up a huge wave. Richard, however, made his way to Collapsible A and was rescued.

▲ *One of Titanic's funnels collapses into the water, as passengers cling onto Collapsible A.*

No more room

As *Titanic* continued to sink rapidly, the people left on board realized they would not be able to get on a lifeboat and were destined to drown with the ship.

FAREWELL

John Jacob Astor helped his young pregnant wife Madeleine onto Lifeboat 4 and asked if he could join her. Officer Lightoller refused, so Astor kissed his wife goodbye and assured her he would board a later boat. Sadly, he didn't manage to get off the ship.

▼ *Madeleine Astor gave birth to John Jacob's son four months after the disaster.*

PARTED BY DEATH

▲ *Isador and Ida Straus. Isador was the owner of Macy's department store in New York.*

Devoted wife Ida Straus, who had been married to her husband Isador for 41 years, refused to leave the ship without him. She helped her maid, Ellen Bird, into Lifeboat 8, handed her a warm fur coat, and stepped back onto the deck to remain on board with her husband. "We have been together all these years," she said to him. "Where you go, I go." They did not survive.

LIFEJACKET THIEF

In the radio room, Jack Phillips frantically sent out distress messages as the ship sank. He was concentrating so hard that he hardly noticed his colleague Harold Bride slide a lifejacket onto him. Bride then left to fetch a spare coat, and as he returned, he saw a stoker trying to steal Phillips' lifejacket. In the ensuing fight, they left the wounded stoker on the floor as they rushed onto the deck. In the end, only Bride survived.

▲ *Phillips made it to the upturned Collapsible B, but he wasn't able to cling on for long enough to be rescued.*

Desperate measures

Not everybody stayed on board and waited for the waves to come. Some men jumped into lifeboats as they were being lowered—in one case, breaking the ribs of the woman he landed on. Others tried to swim to the lifeboats once in the sea.

◄ Bruce Ismay (right) inspecting Titanic with the Chairman of Harland & Wolff, William Pirrie, before the launch.

ROOM FOR THE BOSS

White Star's chairman Bruce Ismay helped many passengers onto the lifeboats. As the waters rose, he eventually boarded Collapsible C. "There were no passengers left on the deck...and as the boat was in the act of being lowered away, I got into it," he said later. Others claimed he pushed his way on board, and he was fiercely criticized for saving his own life when he knew many passengers were going to die.

GENTLEMEN

According to one story, Benjamin Guggenheim stood on the tilting deck, in the freezing night air, with his valet Victor Giglio, both dressed in their finest suits, and said: "We have dressed in our best, and are prepared to go down like gentlemen."

PAYING FOR SAFETY?

On Lifeboat 1, Sir Cosmo Duff-Gordon promised to pay the Titanic crew members £5 each to cover the cost of what they had lost. But later, some people said he made the offer only to stop the crew from rowing back and risking the boat being swamped by desperate survivors.

▶ Sir Duff-Gordon's lifeboat could seat 40 people, but was launched holding just 12.

Three tiny dogs were carried onto the lifeboats: two Pomeranians and a Pekinese.

Final moments

As the last two collapsibles were swept into the sea, *Titanic*'s front funnel fell off, creating a huge wave that washed boats away from the ship. Now the bow sank into the sea and *Titanic*'s lights flickered and went out.

THE BREAK-UP

The pressure on the hull was too much and the ship broke in two with a noise that sounded like an explosion. The bow, already full of water, immediately sank into the depths. The stern started to tip up and the contents of the ship—cargo, fittings, and engines—cascaded into the ocean.

THE FINAL DROP

The stern descended so slowly into the water that chief baker Charles Joughin said: "I was able to straddle the starboard rail (on A Deck) and stepped off as the ship went under... At no time was my head underwater." He swam to the upturned Collapsible B.

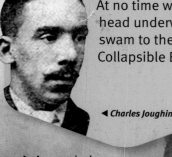

◄ *Charles Joughin*

► *An engraving by the German artist Willy Stöwer, showing the stern sinking into the sea.*

STERN LEFT BEHIND

While the bow sank, the stern settled in the sea for a moment. The terrified people still on board briefly thought that it might stay afloat and they would survive. But then it tipped up to stand almost upright in the water. The passengers tried to cling on as the sudden movement turned the deck into a steep, slippery slope.

WHIRLPOOL

First-class passenger Archibald Gracie was also on the stern as it went down: "Before I could get to my feet I was in a whirlpool of water, swirling round and round, as I still tried to cling to the railing as the ship plunged to the depths below. Down, down, I went." But he was a strong swimmer, and made it back to the surface where he managed to board Collapsible B.

◀ *Gracie wrote a book about* Titanic, *which was published after his death in December 1912.*

RETURN JOURNEY

Most lifeboats didn't go back for survivors. But, about an hour after the sinking, Fifth Officer Harold Lowe transferred people from his lifeboat to another vessel and rowed back to the scene. He found just a handful of survivors amid a sea of dead bodies floating in their lifejackets.

SPINNING UNDERWATER

Jack Thayer decided to jump. "The shock of the water took the breath out of my lungs," he said. "Swimming as hard as I could in the direction which I thought to be away from the ship, I finally came up with my lungs bursting, but not having taken any water." He was dragged into a nearby lifeboat.

▶ *Jack Thayer*

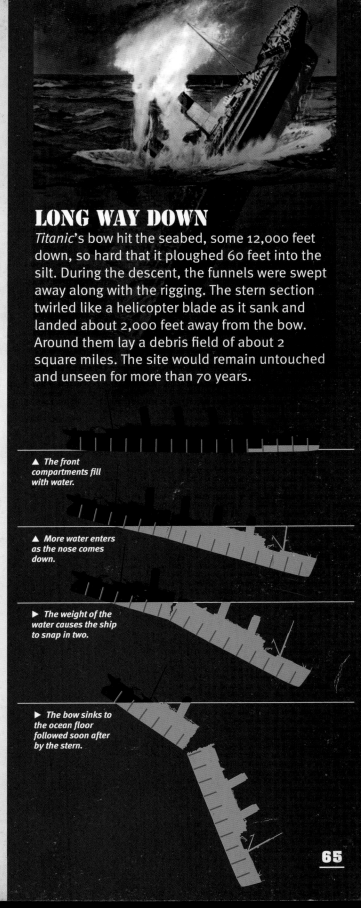

LONG WAY DOWN

Titanic's bow hit the seabed, some 12,000 feet down, so hard that it ploughed 60 feet into the silt. During the descent, the funnels were swept away along with the rigging. The stern section twirled like a helicopter blade as it sank and landed about 2,000 feet away from the bow. Around them lay a debris field of about 2 square miles. The site would remain untouched and unseen for more than 70 years.

▲ *The front compartments fill with water.*

▲ *More water enters as the nose comes down.*

▶ *The weight of the water causes the ship to snap in two.*

▶ *The bow sinks to the ocean floor followed soon after by the stern.*

The aftermath

The survivors endured a freezing night in the open boats. However, they were able to tell a tale that became a global sensation. Soon after the disaster, the US and British governments established inquiries to find out what had caused the sinking— and to prevent something similar from happening in the future.

LIGHTS AND ICEBERGS

The crew tied some of the lifeboats together and transferred occupants from those that were too full to ones that had spare places. Other boats drifted away and were scattered over a nearly 4-mile area. Freezing, frightened passengers lit candles and burned papers to signal for help. Seven-year-old Eva Hart recalled: "As the daylight came we saw the horizon was ringed with icebergs. They looked like beautiful white-sailed yachts."

A CHILD'S VIEW

Six-year-old Douglas Spedden was in Lifeboat 3 with his mother and nanny Elizabeth Burns, whom he called "Muddie" because he couldn't say her name properly. He woke up at dawn, saw many icebergs on the great wide sea, and cried: "Oh, Muddie, look at the beautiful North Pole with no Santa Claus on it."

KEY EVENTS

April 15, 1912
12:25 a.m.: *Carpathia* receives *Titanic*'s distress calls and heads to the disaster zone (see page 67).

April 15, 1912
4:10 a.m.: *Carpathia* arrives, picking up its first survivors from Lifeboat 2 (see page 67).

April 15, 1912
8:30 a.m.: The final lifeboat, Collapsible B, reaches *Carpathia*—706 survivors are now on board (see page 68).

April 15, 1912
8:30 a.m.: *Californian* arrives at the scene, but is too late to help the rescue effort (see page 69).

TO THE RESCUE

Titanic's survivors were collected by one ship, *RMS Carpathia*. It had set off from New York on April 11, taking 743 passengers on a cruise. As soon as its captain, Arthur Henry Rostron, received *Titanic*'s first distress call, he turned his ship around and raced the 58 miles to the troubled liner.

▶ **Captain Arthur Rostron**

▼ *Captain Rostron ordered that Carpathia's heating system be switched off, so as much steam as possible could be used by the engines, making the ship travel much faster than normal.*

ROWING TO SAFETY

Once *Carpathia* reached the disaster zone, it slowed down to dodge ice and to make sure it did not collide with the lifeboats. The first lifeboat, Lifeboat 2, came alongside at 4:10 a.m. Slowly the other boats spotted the ship and rowed toward it.

▲ Titanic *survivors approaching* Carpathia.

▲ *A Titanic lifeboat is lifted aboard* Carpathia.

April 18, 1912
Carpathia is greeted by a crowd of thousands as it arrives in New York (see page 68).

April 19, 1912
The first of two inquiries into the disaster begins in the USA (see page 70).

May 14, 1912
The first film about the story is released, starring *Titanic* survivor Dorothy Gibson (see page 73).

September 1, 1985
The wreck of *Titanic* is discovered after more than 70 years (see pages 74–75).

Pulled from the sea

One by one, the freezing, frightened occupants of *Titanic*'s lifeboats climbed ladders or were winched up on a chair sling onto *Carpathia*. It was four hours before the last boat, Collapsible B, came alongside the rescue vessel.

▲ *A group of* Titanic *survivors aboard* Carpathia *try to come to terms with what had happened.*

AT LAST

Seven hundred and six survivors crammed onto *Carpathia*. They roamed the decks, searching for their loved ones. Some cried with joy when they were reunited with husbands, friends, and relatives. But many realized for the first time that their loved ones were dead. *Carpathia*'s crew and passengers gave the survivors blankets, hot drinks, and spare clothes.

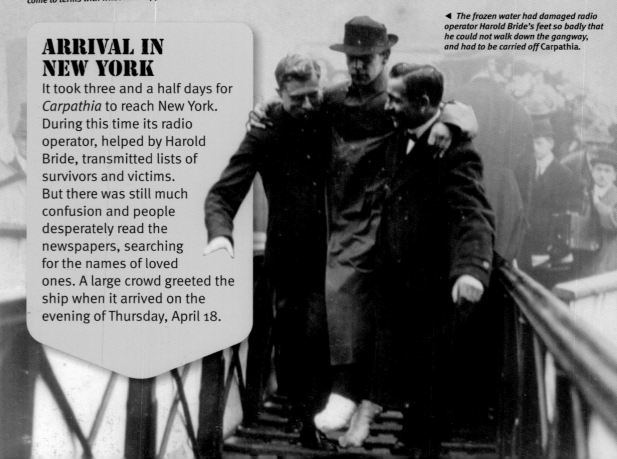

◄ *The frozen water had damaged radio operator Harold Bride's feet so badly that he could not walk down the gangway, and had to be carried off* Carpathia.

ARRIVAL IN NEW YORK

It took three and a half days for *Carpathia* to reach New York. During this time its radio operator, helped by Harold Bride, transmitted lists of survivors and victims. But there was still much confusion and people desperately read the newspapers, searching for the names of loved ones. A large crowd greeted the ship when it arrived on the evening of Thursday, April 18.

Could *Californian* have helped?

Many people on *Titanic* reported seeing the lights of another ship in the distance, and Captain Smith told lifeboat crews to row toward it. That ship was probably *Californian*. It may have been as close as 10 miles, having stopped for the night in the middle of the ice field.

▲ A photo of SS Californian *taken from the deck of* Carpathia *on the morning of the disaster.*

The Californian *was sunk by a German torpedo in World War I.*

NO RADIO CONTACT

Californian's radio operator, Cyril Evans, sent out various ice warnings on the evening of April 14. But he was told off by *Titanic*'s Jack Phillips for interrupting him as he tried to send passenger messages. Evans went to bed at 10 p.m., leaving the radio unattended. *Californian*'s officers saw *Titanic*'s flares, but the captain claimed these were greetings between ships and chose not to wake up the radio operator.

◄ *Seven-year-old Eva Hart recalled: "I remember saying to my mother, 'Why doesn't that other ship come?' You could see it clearly."*

CAPTAIN LORD

The ship's captain, Stanley Lord, denied that he knew *Titanic* had been close and in distress. At dawn, having been informed of the disaster by another vessel, he sailed toward *Titanic*'s position, but he only reached it at 8:30 a.m., as *Carpathia* was taking the last survivors on board. *Californian* stayed and scoured the water for survivors while *Carpathia* headed off to New York.

► *Captain Lord was heavily criticized after the disaster for not responding sooner.*

The two inquiries

▼ A paper boy holds a banner outside the White Star offices on April 16, 1912.

There were two inquiries into the sinking: one in the USA and one in Britain. Both aimed to find out what had gone wrong and how such a disaster could be prevented in the future.

GREAT LOSS OF LIFE

The total number of people on *Titanic* remains unknown because the tickets and paperwork went down with the ship. The US inquiry claimed there were 2,223 people on board. Only 706 survived the journey, meaning that 1,517 lives were lost. The breakdown was:

Class	Died	Survived
First class	130	199
Second class	166	119
Third class	536	174
Crew	685	214

QUESTIONS

The key questions were:

❧ Was *Titanic* sailing too fast given that there was ice ahead?

❧ Why were so few passengers saved?

❧ How could safety at sea be improved?

❧ Could *Californian* have come to help sooner?

◄ Sir Cosmo Duff-Gordon (see page 63) gives evidence at the British inquiry.

CONCLUSIONS

The recommendations were:

❧ Ships should slow down in ice fields and post more lookouts.

❧ Ships must have enough lifeboat spaces for the people on board, and should carry out regular practice drills of loading and launching the boats.

❧ Radios should run 24 hours a day so no distress calls are missed.

❧ Ships should only fire rockets to ask for help, and these must be colored red.

The bodies of only 306 *Titanic* victims were ever recovered from the water.

◄ *Captain Rostron was awarded the Congressional Gold Medal by the US for his actions during the disaster.*

▲ *Bruce Ismay (at the end of the table) gives evidence at the US inquiry.*

THE CAPTAINS

Captain Rostron of the *Carpathia* was praised for his part in the rescue effort. Captain Lord of the *Californian* received criticism for not doing enough. Opinions were divided over *Titanic*'s Captain Smith. Some said he sailed the ship too fast in dangerous waters. Others said this was normal at the time and that he organized the loading of lifeboats well.

ISMAY DISMAY

Bruce Ismay was heavily criticized. He was said to have encouraged Captain Smith to travel dangerously fast so *Titanic* would complete the journey in a quicker time than *Olympic*. He was also accused of cowardice and selfishness for boarding the lifeboat and saving himself while others remained on the ship. Ismay retired and kept out of the public eye following the inquiry.

▲ *Captain Rostron and his crew were presented with a silver cup by the survivors of* Titanic, *thanking them for their heroism.*

The survivors

Titanic's survivors faced great hardships after the tragedy. Many had lost loved ones, and all had lost money and treasured possessions. Those who were emigrating to the USA were left to cope with even more challenges. They also had to deal with the shock of the event —some never forgot the desperate cries for help of those that perished on that ill-fated night.

◄ *Molly Brown's life was turned into a film musical,* The Unsinkable Molly Brown, *in the 1960s.*

HAPPY ENDING

Professional tennis player Karl Behr boarded *Titanic* to follow the woman he loved, Helen Newsom, whom he wanted to marry. Both survived, having gotten onto Lifeboat 5, the second one to be launched. They were married in March 1913, less than a year after the tragedy.

◄ *Karl Howell Behr was able to continue with his tennis career after the disaster.*

UNSINKABLE

Margaret (also known as Molly) Brown was among the few female survivors who had taken up oars to row a lifeboat. Later, she worked to raise money for those who had suffered huge losses in the sinking. She also became a well-known campaigner for women's voting rights and was later referred to as "the unsinkable Molly Brown."

Just 31.6 percent of the passengers on board *Titanic* survived.

Titanic's cultural legacy

The world avidly followed the *Titanic* drama as it unfolded. The story of the "unsinkable" ship that went under the waves on its maiden journey has since been retold countless times in books, films, and TV programs.

TELLING THE STORY

Several survivors, including Lawrence Beesley and Archibald Gracie, wrote books about the tragedy, while others, such as Edith Rosenbaum and Charlotte Collyer, wrote articles or sold their stories to magazines. The silent film actress, Dorothy Gibson, who also survived the tragedy, starred in a film about the sinking, playing herself and wearing the same clothes she had worn in the lifeboat. Called *Saved From The Titanic*, it was released only 29 days after the sinking.

◀ Poster from the 1953 film about the sinking, A Night To Remember.

◀ Dorothy Gibson in a scene from Saved From The Titanic.

BIG HITS

The *Titanic* story has also been featured in movies released in 1953, 1958, and 1980. The 1997 movie *Titanic* was one of the most successful films ever made, winning 11 Academy Awards (Oscars) including Best Picture. It cost about $200 million to make and involved building 90-percent scale reproductions of parts of the ship.

In 1943, the Nazis made a controversial film about *Titanic* with German heroes and Jewish villains.

Found at last

Titanic lay undiscovered for more than 70 years. This was partly because its exact final location was unknown and also because the sea where it sank was 2 miles deep. It took decades to develop vehicles that could dive that far down. But *Titanic* was not forgotten.

Titanic was found 13.2 miles from the position transmitted by its crew as it sank.

RAISE *TITANIC*

There were many suggestions about how to bring *Titanic* to the surface should it ever be found. These included raising it with electro-magnets or filling the ship with buoyant objects such as balloons, wax, ping pong balls, or ice. But none of these ideas would have proved practical.

WRECK FOUND

In September 1985, a French and American team dragging a deep-sea scanner above the sea bed caught sight of some debris. They realized that *Titanic*'s contents—tons of coal, cargo and luggage, boilers and engines, pianos, and countless possessions—had spread over a wide area. They followed the trail to find the wreck.

▶ A pair of shoes recovered from the wreck of Titanic.

▶ An artist's impression of the Titanic wreck site, showing the submarine Alvin approaching the bow section.

THE FIRST VISIT

In 1986, a team of scientists led by the American Robert Ballard crammed inside a tiny submarine called *Alvin* to dive down and visit the wreck. Equipped with a video camera inside the ship, the team enabled the world to see *Titanic* for the first time in 74 years.

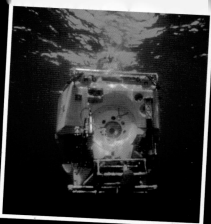

▲ *The submarine* Alvin *begins to descend into the ocean depths to explore the wreck of* Titanic.

FALLING APART

Molluscs have eaten all the wood on *Titanic*, while metal-eating bacteria are working their way through the wreck, leaving behind "rusticles" that hang from the ship. Brass components, such as the propellers, are resistant to this and so will one day be all that is left.

▲ *Long rusticles hang from the front of the ship, eating away the metal.*

SPLIT IN TWO

Ballard had been searching the sea floor for two months before the wreck was found, around 480 miles southeast of Canada in an area now known as *Titanic* Canyon. The wreckage was spread over a wide area, with the bow and the stern lying 1,970 feet apart, facing in opposite directions. This proved that *Titanic* had broken in two before she sank.

MORE VISITS

Since 1985, many dives have been completed to study the wreck, and thousands of objects have been retrieved. These include everything from sections of the hull and passengers' possessions to items of crockery and pieces of coal from the boiler room.

▲ *The deep sea submersible* Mir 1 *is prepared for a dive to* Titanic *in 2003.*

WHO'S WHO?
Titanic

The story of *Titanic* is not just the tale of a giant ship that sank. It is also the 2,223 separate stories of the people on board, including tales of those who acted heroically and those who behaved selfishly, of survivors and victims, some rich, some poor, but all united by that terrible night. Here are some of the most notable figures.

VICTIMS OF *TITANIC*

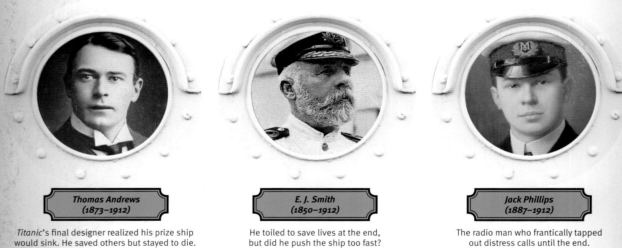

Thomas Andrews
(1873–1912)

Titanic's final designer realized his prize ship would sink. He saved others but stayed to die.

E. J. Smith
(1850–1912)

He toiled to save lives at the end, but did he push the ship too fast?

Jack Phillips
(1887–1912)

The radio man who frantically tapped out distress calls until the end.

Wallace Hartley
(1878–1912)

The musician who led the band as it played to calm frightened passengers.

John Jacob Astor
(1834–1912)

He helped his pregnant wife to a lifeboat, then stayed on the deck.

Benjamin Guggenheim
(1865–1912)

The wealthy man who put on his best clothes and waited to die.

SURVIVORS OF *TITANIC*

**Charles Lightoller
(1874–1952)**

His organization kept Collapsible B
afloat and saved many lives.

**Fred Fleet
(1887–1965)**

The lookout who sounded the
warning about the iceberg ahead.

**Violet Jessop
(1887–1971)**

The nurse who survived the sinking
of both *Titanic* and *Britannic*.

**Cosmo Duff-Gordon
(1862–1931)**

The money he gave to his lifeboat
crew led to accusations of bribery.

**Margaret Brown
(1867–1932)**

She presented a "thank you"
trophy to Captain Rostron.

**Bruce Ismay
(1862–1937)**

The White Star chairman's reputation
was ruined after the disaster.

**Dorothy Gibson
(1889–1946)**

Movie star who survived and appeared
as herself in a film about the disaster.

**Father Francis Browne
(1880–1960)**

The trainee priest whose photographs
survive because he disembarked in Ireland.

**Millvina Dean
(1912–2009)**

A baby on the ship who became
its longest-lived survivor.

GLOSSARY

BERTH
A bed or place to sleep on a ship.

BOW
The front part of a ship.

BRIDGE
The room containing the ship's wheel and navigation equipment, from where the officers control the movement and direction of the ship.

BULKHEAD
A thick wall that divides separate compartments on a ship.

DAVIT
A small crane used for lifting and lowering lifeboats.

DOCKYARD
A place with the facilities to build and repair ships.

DREDGE
To clear mud and other debris from the bottom of a river.

EMIGRANT
Someone who leaves one country to settle permanently in another one.

FIRST CLASS
The section or facilities that are considered the finest and most expensive available.

FLARE
An exploding device, much like a firework, fired into the air to attract attention or call for help.

GENERATOR
A machine that produces—or generates—electricity.

GOLD RUSH
A time when a lot of people suddenly move to an area where gold has recently been discovered.

HULL
The main body, or structure, of the ship, not including its engines, interior fixtures, or masts.

ICEBERG
A very large piece of floating ice that can rise more than 165 feet above sea level and weigh thousands of tons.

IMMIGRANT
Someone who has arrived in another country in order to live there permanently.

KEEL
A long structure that stretches along the bottom of a ship, supporting its framework.

LIFEBOAT
A small boat kept on board a ship and used for evacuating passengers during an emergency.

MAGNATE
A powerful, influential individual in a particular business or industry.

MORSE CODE
A way of communicating in which letters are reproduced using combinations of long and short sounds.

PORT
Refers to both the place where a ship docks and the left-hand side of a ship (when facing the front).

PROMENADE
An open-air walkway, or the act of taking a leisurely outdoor walk.

RADIO
The transmission and receiving of information through the air using electromagnetic waves.

RECIPROCATING ENGINE
A type of engine driven by pistons going up and down.

SECOND CLASS
The section or facilities that are considered the second best available, inferior to first class but superior to third class.

SLIPWAY
A slope, usually made of wood, leading down to an area of water along which a ship is launched.

STARBOARD
The right-hand side of a ship (when facing the front).

STERN
The rear part of a ship.

STEWARD
Someone employed to look after the passengers on a ship.

STOKER
Someone employed to keep a furnace burning by feeding (or stoking) it with fuel.

TENDER
A small boat used to transfer people or supplies to a larger boat.

THIRD CLASS
The section or facilities that are considered the lowest-quality and cheapest available.

TRANSATLANTIC
Crossing the Atlantic Ocean.

TURBINE ENGINE
A type of engine driven by rotating metal blades.

INDEX

Picture credits (t=top, b=bottom, l=left, r=right, c=center, fc=front cover, bc=back cover, i=image)

All images public domain unless otherwise indicated:
Alamy.com: 26tr Stephen Barnes/Titanic, 43c Julia Gavin, 52cl James Nesterwitz, 73bl Lebrecht Music and Arts Photo Library, 74–75b National Geographic Creative. *Dreamstime*: fc line 7 i1, bc line 1 i2, 4cl, 14bl, 15tl, 17cl, 30bc, 44–45b, 54c, 74cl, 77br. *Getty Images*: 12–13b De Agostini Picture Library. *iStock.com*: fc line1 i2, fc line 4 i2, fc line 5 i4, fc line 6 i1, bc line 2, i5. *Shutterstock.com*: fc line 1 i4, fc line 1 i5, fc line 2 i5, fc line 5 i5, bc line 1 i1, bc line 1 i3, fc line 2 i2, bc line 2 i3, bc line 2 i4, bc bl, 12cl, 43cl, 58b, 60–61bl. *Wikimedia Commons*: fc line 4 i4 Digiblue, fc line 5 i6, fc line 6 i5, 23ct, 41cr, 42c, 57cr, Cliff1066, 47tl Prioryman, 48bl InSapphoWeTrust, 48bc Looi.